THE PITKIN REVIEW

Fall 2016

Goddard College
MFA

MISSION STATEMENT

The Pitkin Review is a literary journal produced by writers who are currently enrolled in the MFA in Creative Writing program at one of Goddard College's two campuses: Plainfield, VT or Port Townsend, WA. *The Pitkin Review* is self-supporting, staffed by Goddard MFA candidates, and funded solely by the sales of copies of the publication. *The Pitkin* offers writers experience in submitting to and producing every aspect of a literary journal and also serves as a showcase for exceptional student writing. Published bi-annually in the spring and fall, *The Pitkin Review* is a collaborative community of editors, writers, and graphic artists who volunteer their time and talents to create a high quality publication.

THE PITKIN REVIEW

Fall 2016

Editor in Chief	Will Sweger
Associate Editors	Cara Lang Lena Geneva Smith
Cover Design	Cara Lang
Production Assistant	Tanya Seale
Submissions Editor	Aleesha Nash
Copy Editors	Aaron Kiser Jonathan Ryder Terisa Traylor
Web Chief	Lena Geneva Smith
Business Advisor	Keri Brenning
Social Media	Carleigh Sullivan Carol Harblin
Faculty Liaison	Beatrix Gates
Alumni Advisor	Christine Kalafus
Distribution Manager	Ariel Basom

Lead Editors

Critical Commentary	Sara Cottingham
Cross Genre	Derrick Bergeron
Drama	Sarah Ratermann Beahan
Non-Fiction	Catherine Aarts
Fiction	Anne Boaden
Poetry	Terry Finley
Graphic Novel	Ariel Basom

Genre Editors

Critical Commentary	Catherine Aarts Priya Hajela Aleesha Nash
Cross-Genre	Ariel Basom Tawnya Gyles Carol Harblin
Drama	Mary Cantoral Arianne Goddard Carol Harblin Jon Ulrich

Fiction	Hannah Anderson
	Beth Carbone
	Elizabeth Heckmann
	Bethany Kelly
	Joe Norton
Non-Fiction	Sarah Ratermann Beahan
	Keri Brenning
	Carol Harblin
	Aaron Kiser
	Karen McDonald
Poetry	Catherine Aarts
	Kris Johannesson
	Heather Sargent
	Kristy Watson-Ables
Graphic Novel	Derrick Bergeron
	Tawnya Gyles

CONTENTS

Art

WEB EXCLUSIVES & EDITOR'S PICKS

Fiction
Flyover, An Excerpt | **Sarah Ratermann Beahan**
Red | **Tanya Seale**

Poetry
Riptide | **Sheffield Reynolds**

Art
Robin's Nest | **Jon Ulrich**

These pieces can be found at:
http://blogs.goddard.edu/pitkin

A LETTER FROM THE EDITOR

A story is a living sculpture that slowly reveals itself to the reader. Each scene brings us closer to the whole by showing us another piece of its structure. Through these windows, we enter other worlds that spring from the imaginations of authors.

These pages hold windows to their own worlds, but they are all connected to something larger. Within you will find a community of writers who come together for a short time to pursue their craft in the messy work of creativity. It is the same community of writers that makes this journal possible. The work before you is the result of daydreams, cancelled weekend plans, and nights spent in the dim glow of monitors. More so, it is the result of a group of friends, colleagues, and kindred spirits who come together to support an activity that happens mostly alone.

I am honored to have worked with the fellow writers in this program. Regardless of where their stories take them, the bond we have built in our time together will remain.

I welcome you to the community of writer and reader. I hope the stories revealed on these pages hold as much magic for you as they do for me.

Will Sweger | Editor in Chief

MIRRORS IN CAPE TOWN
Sheffield Reynolds

WHOLE[NESS]
Terisa Traylor

adjective
1. *comprising the full quantity, amount, extent, number,*
   etc., without diminution or exception; entire, full, or total:

what was left behind   was not all
what was left behind   on the table   in the white room
pieces of ourselves   we once loved
lay spoiled

intimate flesh   once animated
now coagulated atop gray steel   isolated

estranged

contrasting the sunset of resolution
with the silvered ocean of loss
the unnatural cold frightening us through
anesthetized slumber

the body always remembers
what the mind would rather forget

2. *containing all the elements properly belonging; complete:*

all that was left behind   calling to us
appendages whispering like ghosts
begging for affirmation   trapped in perpetual
fragmentation
we struggle to rediscover   something whole

to know   that what was left behind was not all
something new   to be born of pieces we shed

3. *undivided; in one piece: to swallow a thing whole*

the expectation of prosthesis   weighs heavy on the
chest
as if   without supplication   we are no longer
all we are

4. *Mathematics. integral, or not fractional. not broken,*
    damaged, or impaired; intact:

scars illustrate the redesign   the regathering of flesh
       to bond stronger   to seal   us up
    the all we once felt   left behind
      in a cocoon stitched of our
      ugly   angry   scars

5. *uninjured or unharmed; sound:*

    waiting for new wings to   burst through
      waiting to be   renewed
   we marvel at the beauty   of necessary chaos
      touch with tender throbbing fingers
places familiar and   freshly foreign
      places rediscovered
    like lovers
rejoicing in the impermeable   the places newly sewn

6. *pertaining to all aspects of human nature, especially one's*
    physical, intellectual, and spiritual development:

    what was left behind   was not all

what was left behind   on the table   in the white room
      pieces of ourselves   and still
      we remain

      we remain still

      something whole

11

NEW AMERICAN GOTHIC
Sheffield Reynolds

CAMDEN YARDS
John Schmidtke
~ *July 30, 1993* ~

I think the ball slipped out of Scott Cooper's hand. Mo Vaughn, at first base, didn't even try to jump; he stood with his right foot loosely toeing the bag and watched the ball sail over his head.

"Heads up," I said to the boys, my voice tight. "Ball coming!"

~ ~ ~

God invented baseball for July afternoons in the mid-80s with a light wind blowing out to left, just active enough to keep the flags awake. We tested God's invention as part of our family's summer trip from Hawaii to the east coast to see as many of Mary's eight sisters as we could squeeze into a two-week vacation. Two sisters lived in Baltimore, and a game at Camden Yards on a Friday afternoon between the home team Orioles and the visiting Boston Red Sox seemed the perfect test event.

The usher had just wiped off our third-row seats in Section 14. The seats faced shallow right field barely past the infield cut. Mary was already sitting down. I still stood, watching the Red Sox take infield practice: Cooper at third, John Valentin at short, Scott Fletcher at second, Vaughn at first, and Tony Pena behind the plate. A coach hit fungos to each fielder, the crack of the ball coming off his bat reaching us with the slightest delay. A grounder to the fielder's left, the catch, the plant, the gather, the throw to first, and then, with another sure crack, a grounder to the fielder's right, the catch, the gather, and the throw to first again, and again, and again: a rhythmic cycle of grace, agility, and power. Vaughn's glove popped with each throw. As the infielders worked on the diamond, the boys stood next me wearing their Hawaii Kai All Star hats—Scott, 10, with his glove on, and Riley, 8, carrying his glove under his armpit. They stared around the nearly new stadium—it opened the season before—at the retro-design, the brick walls, the iron supports, and the green seats filling with the crowd. They looked for Cal Ripken Jr. in the Orioles' dugout. They didn't look at the field.

I watched the Boston coach swing his fungo bat and hit a sharp two-hopper to Cooper's far right, forcing him to backhand the ball in foul territory and to leap, wheel, and throw to first while in the air. That's when the ball slipped out of his hand and sailed over Mo Vaughn's head.

You can't appreciate the power of a major leaguer's arm unless you've been close to the field; TV doesn't capture the deadly speed and air-ripping hiss of a well-thrown ball, and radio only hints at the force of the ball with a distant slap of leather on leather lost behind the announcer's voice. My words made the boys look up, the bills of both their hats pointing at the infield, and when they looked up they saw a well-thrown ball by a major leaguer tearing the air their way. I knew I couldn't make the play without knocking down the boys, but I wasn't sure either boy could catch a ball thrown at major league speed.

~ ~ ~

14

Our Scott has soft, sure hands. As a youth-league catcher he received the ball with nonchalant grace—very few passed balls. As a first baseman he turned lots of poor throws into outs. His first word as a toddler had been "ball." Mary and I played catch with him using tennis balls when he was five and six—we did with Riley, too. When I took Scott to Kokohead District Park to try out for Pinto baseball as a seven-year-old, I walked him from the parking lot to the Pinto field feeling confident and nervous. I knew he was good, but this was his first time throwing and catching in public.

The Pinto League coaches stood on the infield holding clipboards as they watched the boys. The simple tryout started with the boys sprinting from home to first, one after the other. The dads all leaned on the chain-link fence near right field to watch their sons. Next, the boys lined up on the foul line, and one at a time took a defensive stance at first base, glove ready. The Pinto division director rolled the ball from home to first for each boy. Every ball rolled smoothly. Every ball rolled right to the fielder. The boy at first base was supposed to field the ball and then throw to a coach near the pitcher's mound. Scott stood in the middle of the line of about thirty boys.

The ball from the Pinto director went through the first boy's legs. The boy turned, ran into right field, picked the ball up when it stopped rolling, and then heaved it toward second base rather than at the coach near the pitcher's mound. The Pinto coaches wrote notes on their clipboards. I smiled, knowing Scott could field rolled balls easily and knowing he could snap off a throw to the coach's chest. The second kid did the same as the first: he missed the ball, waited for it to stop rolling, picked it up, and threw wildly, with no attempt at accuracy. Each kid did the same. Knowing what I knew, I saw Scott as a potential number one draft pick. I stood shoulder to shoulder with the other dads. I prepared to stay calm, to not react to Scott's play, not wanting to show off when it was my stud kid's turn. I knew Scott would hook the ball into his glove, scoop the ball to his chest, turn his shoulder to his target, crow hop once, and throw the ball on line to the coach.

When his turn came, Scott took his stance. The Pinto director rolled the ball. Scott watched the ball roll between his legs. I straightened up from the fence and gasped. Scott ran after the ball and waited for it to stop. I knew I could barely watch. I started pacing behind the other dads. Scott threw towards second and the ball rolled into left field. I'm sure I turned away. The coaches on the field wrote notes on their clipboards.

"Next!" the Pinto director called. Scott jogged off the field towards me.

"Hey, Buddy!" I said. "Have fun?"

I struggled not to seem disappointed.

"Yeah!"

"Were you nervous?"

"No! It was fun."

"Did the ball take a funny bounce?"

"No."

"Was it too hard?"

16

"No."

I wanted to know what happened. I wanted to know how to fix it. He was just seven-years-old, he seemed to have had fun, and his muffed catch and throw at the tryout didn't seem to bother him. But it bothered me—that ball rolling through his legs, his throw sailing into left. He was so much better than that. Something must have happened. I needed to know. I watched as other fathers walked their sons to the parking lot. Some weren't happy at their sons' performances. They scolded their sons' mistakes. Don't be that dad. The number one rule in youth sports is to have fun. Dads can't let what happens on the field go home in the car. Don't be that dad. Leave what happened here.

"What happened?" I asked Scott as we walked to the car.

"Hunh?"

"The ball got through your legs. What happened?"

"Nothing."

"Nothing?" I asked. "How'd it get through your legs?"

Scott looked at me like I was stupid.

"It was supposed to."

"Hunh?"

"We all did it that way, Dad."

As Scott Cooper's errant throw screamed across the Camden Yards' infield, I wondered whether our Scott could make the play this time.

~~~

But maybe the ball was headed for Riley; it had a slight hook as it closed on us. All year in the regular season, and in the post-season All Stars, Riley had played third—the hot corner they call it in the Bigs, but it's just a tepid position at the Pinto level: no seven- or eight-year-old batter ever yanked a screamer down the left field line. Certainly nothing like the fungo Cooper backhanded in Camden Yards' foul territory.

Riley played baseball for fun. He stopped playing in high school when the coaches forgot the number one rule. He switched sports, and became a state champion wrestler by turning agony and effort into fun. Years after our two boys graduated from college, while Mary and I sat with them at AT&T Park in San Francisco watching the Braves—our team—play the hometown Giants, I asked what their favorite memory had been playing baseball in Hawaii Kai. Both boys had made All Stars at each level. Both boys had made it deep into the state tournaments, losing to teams that fielded future major leaguers.

"Sky Inning," Riley said without any pause.

"What?"

"Sky Inning," Scott agreed.

The kids played Sky Inning into the night after each late afternoon game while the dads turned the post-game potluck for the kids into a twilight outdoor party fueled by Keystone Light, pipikaula, dried squid, ahi poke, and edaname. Each year during the player draft, after getting the best player available in the first round, experienced coaches drafted a kid whose mom or dad sparkled at cooking. One coach always drafted Roy Yamaguchi's son. Roy, a magnificent chef specializing in Pacific-Rim cuisine, founded

Roy's Restaurants—each one of his twenty-two restaurants offers a high-end culinary treat for the palate, and his first opened in Hawaii Kai in 1988. That team ate gourmet potluck with endless, elegant pupus for the dads who stayed late. I always drafted a boy whose dad owned a local favorite, Magoos Pizza (*No Hu-Hus? Call MaGoos!*), and while the kids on my team wolfed pepperoni pizzas, the dad's ate pork belly, olive, avocado, and mozzarella pizzas followed by multi-meat subs late into the night. "Ho, Glenn!" a dad would say between bites. "Dis is broke-da-mouth, bra! I swear! Broke-da-mouth!" The moms normally left the park early to take the younger brothers and sisters home. The dads usually brought home the players.

While the dads ate and drank, taking time between beers to rake the base paths, mow and edge the infield, and water the grass for the next day, the kids played Sky Inning. One kid would bat, and the others would try to get the batter out. Simple. The game worked best on a slight slope. The batter would soft-toss the ball—usually a tennis ball or a soft-core baseball—and hit it in the air with a bat. The other players would try to catch the ball on the fly, giggling and jostling like bridesmaids reaching for an arcing bouquet. If a fielder caught the ball on the fly, the dads would hear a delighted cheer and know the Sky Inning batter was out. The kid who caught the ball would switch places with the batter. If no one caught the ball, the batter would put the bat on the ground and stand behind it. Whoever had the ball would bowl it at the bat. If the ball missed the bat, the batter would keep hitting. The dads knew a missed bat by the groan from the fielders. If the ball hit the bat, it would bounce into the air like a foul tip off the top curve of the bat on a bunt attempt. If the batter caught the ball in the air, the batter would keep hitting. Cheers and groans! If not, the batter would be out, and the bowler would come in to hit. A big cheer! No coaches. No umpires. No practices. Just kids. Pure fun.

One night at the park, much later than usual, I called Scott from Sky Inning, and we drove home. Mary and Riley had left the park long before. I pulled in our garage. Scott headed to the laundry room to take off his uniform. Mary met me at the door.

"Where's Riley?" she said.

Mary and I played a game every time I came home. Even though Riley would come home with her, she'd ask me where he was, and I'd say I didn't know. Riley was probably five, at most. I'd always say I thought he'd come home with her. She'd say he hadn't, and then I'd look all over the house, calling out every time I looked in a new place, "Where's Riley? I can't find him!." He'd be hiding somewhere obvious, but I'd look in closets, look in kitchen drawers, look in the oven, look behind the couch, look in the trash can, look under beds, and each time I looked somewhere new he'd laugh harder until he'd burst out from his hiding place and surprise me. Mary would sell the fake search by answering every time I asked where he was, "I don't know. I thought you had him."

"Where's Riley?" I asked as I came in from

the garage. I looked under the dining room table.

"I don't know," Mary said. "I thought you had him."

"Where's Riley?" I asked, looking behind my recliner.

"I don't know," Mary said again. "I thought you had him."

"Where's Riley?" I asked, looking under one of the cushions on the couch.

Mary grabbed my left shoulder and spun me around. Her clinched jaw surprised me. Her normally warm and patient gray-blue eyes looked icy and urgent. She held both my shoulders.

"Where's my son?"

She wasn't playing a hide-and-seek game. Her youngest was missing. In the days before cell phones, there was no way to call for help.

"I'll be right back," I said.

I drove to the park. I wanted to speed, but I drove under the limit, afraid of being stopped. I pulled in the lower lot and parked.

"John!" the dad's called when I parked. "You're back!"

"Hey, guys! Have you seen Riley?"

Several pointed to the upper parking lot, a long sloped lot, well lit by the outfield lights on the Pony Field. A happy gaggle of kids played Sky Inning. Riley, too young to catch a batted ball and too young to really hit, ran and laughed with the older kids—the joy of the game overcoming any need to excel.

"Looks like Mary's gonna serve someone up some dirty lickin's when you get home, Coach!" one dad called. The rest snorted. I ran up to get

Riley. He didn't want to come home.

"Here's Riley," I said when Mary met us at the garage door. "I found him!"

She didn't think I was funny.

"I was playing Sky Inning, Mom," Riley said as he went in. He sounded proud.

And later, when he started playing baseball, he always made us proud. Riley's hands weren't as soft as Scott's, but he stopped everything hit his way fearlessly, knocked down anything he didn't catch cleanly, and made the play with a powerful, high-elbowed throw. But on that day in Camden Yards, even if Riley's glove had been on his hand rather than under his arm, I had no confidence he could catch Scott Cooper's ball.

~~~

In the slow instant in Camden Yards after I said "heads up," I decided to try for the ball. I could feel Mary gathering to my left, readying herself to protect her boys. I knew I blocked her way. I glanced down, like a first baseman finding the bag, to see whether I could scoot quickly to my right without knocking the boys down and hurting them. But I knew I was coming their way no matter what—a bruise from falling against a seat or a scrape on the knee from skidding on the concrete would hurt or bleed, but getting beaned could be deadly. When I looked down, I paused. I couldn't scoot to my right at all. I couldn't because both boys were on their knees and elbows like supplicants begging mercy, butts up, hands over their heads, the bills of their All Star hats touching the floor, their gloves on the concrete next to them, and both using the seats of

22

Row Two as a shield.

Scott Cooper's errant throw crunched into the back of the seat in front of our Scott. Two inches higher and it would have cleared that seat in Row Two and smacked into Riley's seatback. No way either boy would have caught it. I might have, even barehanded, but it would've hurt. Scott Cooper's ball ricocheted down from the seatback and into the spring-loaded seat itself. The force of the ricochet pushed the Row Two seat down and the seat's springs absorbed the energy of the throw. As the springs pulled the seat up and into place, the ball softly flipped straight up.

~~~

The best in the ballpark showed off at Camden Yards that day. Mo Vaughn might not have been able to catch Scott Cooper's pre-game throw, but in the third inning he jacked a two-run home run. Two years later, Vaughn would hit .300 with thirty-nine homers, and be recognized as the American League's Most Valuable Player. Harold Baines, the Orioles' Designated Hitter, crushed a two out grand slam in the fourth inning. He hit .313 that year. In his twenty-two year career, the six-time All Star would drive in more runs than anyone not in the Baseball Hall of Fame. Andre Dawson, the DH for the Red Sox, the 1977 Rookie of the Year, an eight-time All Star, the 1987 National League's MVP, and a future Hall of Famer, cranked a three-run homer in the first. And the best on the field, Cal Ripkin, Jr., a nineteen-time All Star, a two-time MVP, the 1982 Rookie of the Year, the holder of the most consecutive games played in the history of baseball (2,632), and another member of the Hall of Fame, went deep with a solo shot in the second.

But none of them—not Vaughn, not Baines, not Dawson, and not Ripkin—caught Scott Cooper's ball as the springs of the seat in Row Two flipped it softly in the air. None of their sons, All Star caps askew, looked up at them from the concrete with wide eyes showing a mix of fear, relief, and wonder to see their dad unexpectedly holding a major league baseball. None of their sons thought the ball had been caught barehanded on the fly. And none of their wives looked at them with raised eyebrows that said, "I know what you're thinking. Have your fun for a second—I know you can't help yourself—but you ought to tell your sons the truth."

~~~

God invented baseball for families to enjoy on a July afternoon, the air in the mid-80s, and a light wind blowing out to left, just active enough to make memories.

ATLANTIC FLYING
Sheffield Reynolds

THE FRAGILE IMAGINATION OF EMPATHY
Terisa Traylor

Family
Honor
Home

Do you not remember
How sweet the air tastes
When you wake up
Whole
Body un broken
Children not puckered with blood
dotted with stained pits wheezing smoke
Shrapnel still solid
Family and home safe from the splinters of war
Your honor the only casualty

Do you not remember
The beast of hunger coiling around the center
of your distended belly
Placating itself with the pieces of stone and clay
you have ground and swallowed your memory
of flesh with a mouth dry and
deserted

Do you not remember that once your pen could
not meet paper

Besides to make lists
Collections of things to fill the needs
of the oppression that kept you mute
Categorized and restricted
Labeled insane by the bitter fear of strangers
Creativity and clitoris castrated
Systemically lobotomized until you
could not remember

Do you not remember the chains that bound
your words
Free only to write propaganda
Steel licking your pale and
throbbing neck a consequence of the
image you drew
line you wrote
thought you felt
Not even your deepest emotions
given the privilege of   feeling

You only remember the life you've known
Grieve only for the losses
Large and small/ never anyone's
But your own

We cannot ask you if enough has been
had if you have always refused to
swallow
what isn't yours

You said the bread tastes sour
and the wine   pungent
the magic unconvincing
yet you gorge yourself between the wooden pews
so the guilt can be bottled up and given back
washed clean so that you
Do not remember

Family
Honor
Home

EXCERPT FROM "SOUL CANDY"
Jalyn Powell

Condensation dripped down the side of Anton's cocktail glass in alternating reflections of chartreuse, teal, and violet. The bar's ambient lights transitioned among the three shades in a sad attempt to mimic the exclusive clubs in Haven Hill.

It reminded him of one of those archaic disco balls lighting up an empty dance floor: the party-goers too despondent to rise from their seats, too apathetic to even speak, and fuzzy elevator music rambling in the background. The drink itself was supposed to be a Roulette cocktail, the preferred beverage of Haveners, but the bitter concoction in front of him was a poor-man's imitation. Its mood-modifying technology barely registered in his bloodstream.

Still, it was the best he could get in this part of Midtown. Or any part of Midtown.

With a resigned sigh, Anton sucked it down and slammed the empty glass on the chipped laminate counter. A hint of happiness sparked in his mouth, but as soon as he swallowed, the weakly engineered mood effect was gone. He looked at the bartender, dejectedly. Every day for the past six months, he'd been observing the man's white shirt gradually darken to a depressing shade of piss.

The bartender, whose name was something like Tommy or Troy, asked, "Top you off?"

Anton studied his empty glass and then his

mood-tech ring. It was black, the color of despair, or perhaps indifference. "You said this was a Roulette, right? I might as well be drinking regular vodka. I don't feel any emotions mixed in."

"We don't carry Soul Candy liquor. This stuff is a knock-off. Spirit Water."

"Spit water?"

"Funny. Try taking off your mood-tech when you drink. It spoils the fantasy."

Anton scoffed at the man's advice, but he couldn't help glancing behind him to the scattered tables of Mids, swirling tiny straws in their colorless drinks. They sat together with walls up, forcing smiles after each sip to convince themselves, and each other, of their happiness. Like Toby suggested, he didn't see any mood-tech on their fingers or around their necks. They probably thought they *were* happy.

Anton knew better, though.

Just yesterday, he had been waiting for the Midtown train to take him from one end of the concrete city to the other, one identical building to the next, one sterile box to another, when the sleek and shining train to Haven Hill darted high above him. He had thought about climbing up the scaffold base of the soaring tracks and waiting for the next one to fly past, to grab hold, and ride it to paradise. His mood-tech ring had turned a hopeful shade of periwinkle at the thought of escaping to Haven Hill, but then a body plummeted from the sky and landed next to him with a sickening crunch on the platform. The woman's blood and brain matter had splattered on Anton's shoes. His ring had returned to its

30

normal temperament of black as he shook the sticky remains from his clothes. It wasn't the first time a Mid or Sewie woke up from the fog of meaningless life and attempted the escape. But if Anton were to muster up the courage and try to catch a ride, by god, he wouldn't let go till he got there.

"I prefer reality," he said to Trent and watched him pour the bottom-shelf mood liquor in the glass. Its opaque coloring suggested dirty water.

"Reality is overrated, my friend," said a voice behind him.

Anton turned to see a man in a fashionable white leather jacket, the kind that cost a thousand bucks to get tailor-made, grinning at him. His teeth were almost as white as his clothes, and an alluring woman in a corseted burgundy dress hung on his arm. Flecks of gold covered her cheekbones, eyelids, and lips like a trail of stars leading to heaven.

Haveners.

The man wore black sunglasses that shielded any sign of his eyes. Without invitation, he sat down at the bar next to Anton, and the woman remained standing behind her date with hands draped over his shoulders and chest. Her eyes never left Anton. They glittered as gold as her skin. He'd heard Haveners sometimes wandered down from Haven Hill, but he'd never seen them up close before. They were even more brilliant than the commercials: *Rise to Haven Hill,* the ads proclaimed next to glamorous shots of glitzy condos and skyscrapers piercing the clouds. *Feel the Paradise.*

The male Havener stuck out a perfectly manicured hand and said, "The name is Blaze."

He grasped it with his own clammy one. "Anton."

"I came over here because I noticed your mood-tech. Not many Midtowners wear them."

"Keeps me honest, I guess." He fidgeted with his ring, cleared his throat, and wished he'd shaved recently. He didn't even know the last time he'd done laundry. The angelic vision of the Haveners compared to his dark and disheveled state made it painfully obvious who was blessed and who was damned.

"It suits you," said Blaze, looking him up and down and nodding approvingly. "Like a true Havener: unafraid of feeling."

Anton felt his cheeks burn at the compliment, but after a few seconds, the blush died. There was no way he could be confused for a Havener. He only had a hundred bucks to his name and a dead-end job inputting numbers in endless columns and rows that no one would ever look at. He felt nothing. "Thanks, but I'm no Havener. I've only got one mood most days."

"Would you like more?" asked Glitter Girl. Her golden eyes were honey.

Anton quickly looked away. "I wouldn't know what to do with them," he said as he downed the already warm pseudo-Roulette. Toilet water, he thought. Nothing but toilet water and tears.

"I'm throwing a party tonight," said Blaze. "Why don't you come?"

Anton stared from Blaze to Glitter Girl to Todd (or whatever the bartender's name was). The bartender raised his eyebrows, equally shocked. Anton stuttered: "To Haven Hill?"

Blaze stood up magnanimously with a wink and a smile. "Where else? And I only serve the finest Roulettes." He motioned for Glitter Girl to give Anton an oversized card she had produced from her purse.

As she stepped closer, he reflexively straightened up, heart quickening and palms sweating. She leaned down low and whispered in his ear, "I can't wait to see you again." Their hands touched when he took the card. Glitter Girl's nails sparkled in the dim light like a vein of gold in a dark cavern, and his ring faded from black to periwinkle as he took the offering.

Control the tech. He managed a polite smile as he willed the color of hope away. He wasn't afraid to feel, but there was a time and a place. And how pathetic was he to show his desperation so easily? Haveners weren't salivating over party invitations and beautiful women. They weren't weak.

"Sure, I'll think about it," he said in the smoothest voice he could muster.

"I don't hand those tickets out to just anyone," Blaze said as he straightened his immaculate jacket and adjusted his shades. "And it's for tonight only, you understand."

Then he shook Anton's hand in farewell and walked out of the bar with Glitter Girl latched onto his arm. She sneaked a final, lingering look before the door shut behind them.

As if a switch had been pressed, the usual

Midtown darkness crept back into everything –
the shadows grew blacker, the air grew staler – as
if radiance followed the Haveners wherever they
tread, and only once it was gone did you realize
how bleak and dreary the world really was.

Despite the melancholic aura, an invigorating
tingle danced inside him, stronger than any mood
the imitation Roulette could ever claim to provide.
He looked at the card. The ornate calligraphy was
written in gold ink that shimmered like Glitter
Girl's lips. *Admit One to Haven Hill.*

"If you don't want to go to the party, I'll buy
that ticket from you," said Travis as nonchalantly
as possible, wiping down the permanently stained
and peeling counter. When Anton didn't respond,
he said: "C'mon, this one's on me," and filled his
glass with yet another transparent cocktail of
bland oblivion.

Anton could probably get a couple thousand
for the invite, but he would be back to broke soon
enough. The Mids might not even believe it was a
bona fide Haven Hill ticket if he showed them.
They would laugh at his gullibility. But when
would he get another chance to see the shining
city?

"What's your name, anyway?" Anton asked.

"Tyler."

Anton nodded to himself. He had known it
started with a T. He held the invitation in one
hand and the cocktail in the other, eyeing the
sweating glass. Blobs of ice swam on top. It
reminded him of backwash. He pushed it away
and carefully placed the ticket in his wallet so it
wouldn't crease.

"Thanks for the offer, but I've got a train to catch."

END SCENE

TRIUMPHANT
Terisa Traylor

Evil:

> Waits in the wing;
> sits patient;
> takes up hobbies; sustains itself
> playing idly with your time
> you   won't give,
> your   blood you   won't shed;
> while you take solace in small

Triumphs.

> ~~Unaware~~ Heedless to what lurks
> in the shadows,
> you hide in plain sight.
> The personal place where you feel
> value   /   meaning.
> Glory that does not translate.
> The individual concerned with
> his lonely singular cause.

Only,

> no man is an island.
> No woman a country despite
> we   calling   her   mother...
> Out of ~~love~~ loyalty.
> They   are
> not   the same.
> And only one will
> command the other.   It is only

When

> you sweat for a gain that is not your own.
> You bleed to heal a wound
> that is not your own. When

you fight in a war you believe
is not your own,
because you cannot stand by
and watch

Good

be slaughtered by the wealth of
indifference. The community stripped of
its pluralism, left naked and shamed
alone   in   the   street
struggling   to   breathe...
begging for the mercy of

Men,

but find only beasts.
And you, with all the power
the sword quivering in your ready hand...
have let the silence be your only mirror.

Do

you not hear it screaming?
A monster fed upon your idle time.
Bred in the places where you have done

Nothing.

NEAR THE CLOWN MOTEL
Sheffield Reynolds

IFS, ANDS, AND BUTTS
Annie Galligan

I collect things with big butts. This was accidental at first, and came about when I found a wooden figurine at a flea market. She was a faceless lady with the wind blowing up her skirt like it did Marilyn's. Her dress was orange instead of white, her hair an unruly black puff instead of blond ringlets. She had giant hoop earrings, and best of all, an ass that so overtook the rest of her frame, resting her against the wall was the only way her seller could keep her standing.

In the doll's empty space for eyes, I stared back at me. A girl with a fondness for bright colors, a love of hoochie-hoops and, most importantly, a rear end that monopolizes the eye. So I spent 80 cents at that flea market, brought her home in my back pocket, and placed her prominently on a shelf at the top of the stairs.

Later, during a trip to Pier One, my roommate pointed out a piggy bank displaying a rump that was abnormally endowed compared to that of its displayed compadres. In fact, it was so strangely formed that the clerk sold it to me for half price saying, "how on earth did that happen?"—a question that I've often asked about my own casting.

With time the collection has grown along with my own derriere. There's a Kim Kardashian action figure, an abnormally proportioned fake rifle, and a pack of Camel Wides that really just look like trash because they were smoked in drunken desperation long ago. There's a picture of George W. Bush, and one of a donkey wearing pajamas, and even the box from a 12-stick pack of butter with a perfectly positioned discount sticker that hides the 'e' and the 'r'. The collection of butts suits my appearance, and it aims to convey that I am comfortable in my own skin; able to celebrate my extra padding; able to denounce anyone who might be critical of my body as an ass.

But there's also a mirror on that shelf, and in it lurks a whole other collection. It is far too easy to remove the extraneous 't's—to see *buts* that are much uglier than my fat ass could ever be. *Buts* and *ifs*, *ifs* and *whys*, *whys* and *how comes*, and the *hows* of how I came to be a woman so eager for visual proof that I am all right as me.

There's a very fine line between reason and excuse, and a very fine chance, that at any given moment, you won't find me flailing my arms, teetering between the two. Some hide it in their closets, some bury it in dalliance, but I flaunt my illness like Kardashian waves her assets in front of the camera. I want you to know why I'm unable to maintain eye contact and why I can't leave the scabs on my face alone. I want you to know why I left the hair dryer in the fridge, and the milk in the laundry hamper. I want you to know why I develop shaky hands and shaky memory in the afternoon, and why I started crying when you asked me to choose the restaurant where we should eat. I want you to know why it's been days since I brushed my teeth, and why I need you to write Facebook posts without grammatical errors,

40

and why I woke up in a crack house in Maryland last year and why I haven't held a job for ten years and why none of my sweatpants have strings and why my hair is falling out, and why I stayed up for three days and why I slept for three days, and why I spent $400 on pens and why my ass will never stop getting bigger, and why I'm so unreliable and so untrustworthy. I want you to know all of this because I want you to know you can trust me.

I want you to know that I am not just quirky. I am not just spontaneous. I am not a free spirit or free thinker speaking her mind. I am not just overtired, I am not just overworked. I am not being creative or being imaginative or being sensitive or being silly or being reasonable, or even being me. I'm not even sure I can conjure what it was like to be other than just an excuse for me.

The problem with moving past years tarnished by debilitating mental illness, is that there is a debilitating desire to keep them in the past. To speak of that time as something over which I've triumphed, a thing that deserves a certain amount of appreciation because a huge-assed phoenix has arisen from those ashes, and can speak about it with a smile. I portray the existence of a woman whose life is a redemption. A life that is worth sharing. A life that she is proud of, that silences whispers, and assigns strength to the scars. But sharing so much of where I've been denies the possibility, and likely probability, that you will find me there again. That a pill could lose its influence, a jarring trauma could loosen a screw. I cling to the idea that I have traveled a linear path and reached the final destination of sanity. But this is a place I've visited before, and to think I won't eventually wear out my welcome is insane.

So I search for absolution with explanations. I would look you in the eye while you're speaking, but I must maintain a focal point to avoid distraction by the words only I can hear. I would have a lovely complexion, but the drive to unclog grimy pores is stronger than the drive to be attractive for the man I love. The hairdryer would be in the bathroom drawer, but I got lost in that world where I forgot to shut off the stove and everyone I love burned down around me. My hands would be steady, but my lithium level is too high, and food is the only thing that helps, but choosing a restaurant could mean my choice led to the wiry hair in your mashed potatoes. My teeth would be brushed, but you used the 'there' when it should have been 'their' and I've been checking every Facebook post I've made in five years to make sure I haven't made the same mistake. And I wouldn't have gone to that crack house in Maryland, but they all just seemed so nice at the time, and I'd be a lawyer or a professor or a stay-at-home mom, but no benefit package or list of maternal expectations includes months of vacation time in a psych ward. My pants would have strings but the doctors were worried I might hang myself, and my hair would be thick and full, but they can't get the dosage right, and I would sleep but there's just so much to do and think and say, and I would wake up, but there's just so much to do and think and say, and I wouldn't have maxed out my credit card at Staples, but there is a perfect marriage of pen and paper that I simply must find, and if the antipsychotics hadn't killed my metabolism, I would be able to lose weight, and I would have a smaller ass. I would be reliable. I would be trustworthy. I say this, but I know you cannot trust me.

I am just tired. I am just ashamed. I am scattered and confused and lost in a solitary mirage that looks nothing like what I see. I have erected a tower that is barely strong enough to brandish a flag of victory for a battle that was won long ago. A fight that nearly killed me, but a mere skirmish in comparison to the wars left to come.

I am gazing at myself in the mirror, at my yellow dress and hoop earrings. I am gazing in the mirror at a big butt, but even bigger *buts*, and because of that, nothing seems to fit.

WAITING AT A MOTEL 6
Sheffield Reynolds

THEN ARJUNA ASKED
Laura Schaeffer

Atman, if you can save me,
     This little fog will pass
then tell me how to lose shadows
     it is nothing but an eyelid
attached to my feet
     closed over a green vase
or the mimicry of each warrior's act
     where
echoing behind and before me now.
     the bloom and drinking stem lived

My dharma divides between fear and love.
     so fragrant
My sword is double-edged.
     in an old room.

SOMETHING IN COMMON
Tanya Seale

A coffin contains a woman in a funeral parlor,
with three or four chairs and a guest book nearby.
We cannot see woman except for two large
mounds of breast tissue, which rise up over the
side of the coffin. HENRY, a handsome gray-
haired man, dressed in a smoking jacket, sits in
one of the chairs, mourning the death of his
beloved BELLA. Bella's professionally dressed
but estranged grown children, JAMES and
ELIZABETH, arrive and enter the viewing room.

JAMES

Hi. Are you…

HENRY

(Rising to greet them.)

Henry. Henry Rollins. Greetings.

JAMES

Henry Rollins? No kidding?

HENRY

Not *the* Henry Rollins, obviously. I like to think
I'm a much more ahh… dignified sort of fellow.

James eyeballs the smoking
jacket.

JAMES

Yes, I can see that you think that. I'm Bella's son.
James. James Taylor. And this is my sister,
Elizabeth.

HENRY

James and Elizabeth Taylor. Well then...

(Chuckles pretentiously.)

We all have something in common.

Elizabeth looks at James
uneasily but shakes
Henry's hand with extreme
reverence.

ELIZABETH

My deepest sympathies, Mr. Rollins.

James takes Henry in and
looks to Elizabeth for
concurrence.

JAMES

I hardly think we have much in common, but I
appreciate your sense of humor.

Elizabeth punches James.

JAMES

(Whispering to Elizabeth.)

What? Look at him. He looks like Hugh Hefner.

HENRY

(Clears throat.)

Well, at any rate, I am pleased to *finally* make your acquaintance. I know it was a great disappointment to my lovely Bella that the two of you couldn't make it for Christmas. Or for Thanksgiving. Or for her birthday. Or Easter before that.

JAMES

No need to play hardball, Mr. Rollins. I am certain, you being a man so... full of life experience and all, that you might understand the demands of a career. Life just... you know...gets in the way... sneaks up on you and... *surgeons* are frequently on call. Most all the time really... so it isn't always convenient or emotionally effective to come running every time Mother sheds a crocodile tear.

HENRY

No, I don't suppose it is, young man. I don't

believe she made any demands on you that you weren't willing to dismiss.

ELIZABETH

We both have incredibly demanding jobs, Mr. Rollins.

JAMES

Yes, and what is it *you* do again? Besides travel abroad?

HENRY

(Biting the end off a cigar.)

Rest assured I have heard it all before. I have children of my own. Time gets away from you and then before you know it...

> Henry whistles and makes a shot to the temple, then closes his eyes as if he's dead.

ELIZABETH

It's just that it's so hard when careers and families and... James lives clear on the other side of town. And I'm all the way out in the suburbs...

(Realizing her excuses are flimsy.)

You know *you all* could have come out to see us too.

HENRY

I suppose.

JAMES

(Melodramatically.)

God, I miss her already.

> Elizabeth comforts
> James.

ELIZABETH

It's always difficult to know what to say under these circumstances. But rest assured we are truly very sorry for your loss.

HENRY

And I for yours.

ELIZABETH

Thank you.

> They all sit, uncomfortably
> for a moment. Henry
> lights up, so Elizabeth
> coughs, and then, in an
> attempt to dodge the

smoke, she decides to view the body. She pulls out a trinket that she plans to leave with her mother, a handkerchief or quilt square. Her mouth opens and closes and then opens again.

ELIZABETH

Um. Mr. Rollins?

(Pointing.)

Whose boobs are those?

James bolts from his seat to have a look too.

HENRY

That is your mother, Bella. Of course that is also Bella's bosom.

ELIZABETH

No. That is not Bella's bosom. Whose *boobs* are those?

JAMES

(Gasps.)

Dear God in heaven above. Whose lips? Whose nose job is that? Oh! Mother! You didn't!

ELIZABETH

(Agitated.)

She did! The boobs! Who did the boobs?

JAMES

Forget the boobs. Look at the botox! You've made her into some sort of twice baked playboy bunny. Our mother! Our respectable, matronly mother!

HENRY

Your mother quite liked the "boobs."

ELIZABETH

With all due respect, Mr. Rollins, those are not *boobs*.

(Points to her own.)

These are boobs. *Those* are knockers. Jugs. Badungadungas.

JAMES

Our father is rolling in his grave right now. Our mother bought herself some fun bags. And...

(Noticing these now too.)

...hair plugs! What else did she have done?

> He lifts the lower half of
> the casket.

JAMES, CONT.

Mother! Henry Rollins! How could this happen?
Don't tell me she spent our entire inheritance on
this!

ELIZABETH

James!

JAMES

I still have student loans, Liz. Don't tell me you
weren't thinking the same thing. And now! Now
I realize we probably owe every other plastics guy
in the state for this... this piece of work.

> Elizabeth touches the
> boobs, squeezes them.

ELIZABETH

Mother! These boobs are so... so...

> She peers down Bella's
> shirt.

ELIZABETH, CONT.

Oh for God's sake.

HENRY

I can't believe you wouldn't support your
mother's dying desire. She felt beautiful and she
was beautiful because of it.

ELIZABETH

Because she had Grand Tetons?

HENRY

Because they made her feel beautiful! I can't
believe you, as a woman, don't understand that!

JAMES

I can't believe you don't think it's preposterous!
An elderly woman spending all her money and
probably ours too, now, on this. This!

ELIZABETH

(Crossing arms.)

Well *I* can't believe she went to *him*! Dr. Allen P.
Wyndham. I would know his boob work
anywhere.

HENRY

You're not the only plastics specialists in town,
Drs. Taylor and Taylor.

JAMES

I beg your pardon. I am a burn specialist, Mr.
Rollins. I do not perform unnatural and
unnecessary "beauty" enhancements to grown
peoples' *mothers*.

ELIZABETH

(Shooting James a dirty look.)

And I beg your pardon as well. There's enough
work here for ten surgeons. How many did she
have? How many, Henry? Two? Three? Six?
Twelve? Did they all know about each other? Did
they? Did they all know about *us*? That she was
our mother?

HENRY

She only had the one, my dear Elizabeth.

Elizabeth embraces James.

ELIZABETH

Wyndham?

HENRY

He knew her by the name "Bunny." No first. No
last. Just "Bunny." She paid in cash. Wore a scarf
into and out of his office so no one would see
her.

ELIZABETH

And she loved him?

HENRY

Indeed. He treated her well. Just look at her.

JAMES

And he's paid in full?

HENRY

Every last penny.

JAMES

Thank God!

ELIZABETH

Yes! Thank God!

HENRY

I was just sitting there thinking the same thing.

56

Before you walked in. I was just thinking the same thing! I was thinking thank God. Thank God for women like Bella Taylor.

JAMES

Well then. Perhaps we do have something in common.

ELIZABETH

Perhaps we do.

> Their phones start buzzing and beeping.

ELIZABETH

I have to go. I have to go perform an emergency butt lift.

JAMES

Me too. Scheduled dermabrasion on a teen boy who can't get a date to save his life.

HENRY

Nice meeting the two of you. I hope you'll be at the funeral. But just in case, don't forget to sign the guest book on your way out. Your mother will want to know you were here.

> Blackout. End of play.

BY MOONLIGHT
Johnathan Ryder

Tonight the air smells
of lavender and blood.
Howls ring like an orchestra,
simple symphony not meant
for man or woman.
Yet the brave, young and foolish,
slip from their sleep
pulled past the point of safety.

Try to find our secrets
within the day's inky sibling.
Sniff the air
and see the colors.
Feel the deceptive ground
as it gives way with each step,
the crunch of branch and bone
letting us know you.

Unwavering eyes shine
with teeth ready to bare
and limbs loose to chase.
I could a tale for you unfold
of Eden and apples
and gods forced to kneel
or I could tear
into your fleshy shell
to feed my family,
free you to find a new road.
You who are blind to what you seek,
looking for meaning

or lack there of.

When it is not the
meaning that matters
but everything else.
So step within our night,
O brother and sister,
and see for yourself.

FEBRUARY
Lucy A. Snyder

click! click! click! click!
mammary mammogram Mammon
female meat modestly stripped
medical glass manly gods
little tin lover boy
       Let's just be friends
snot stomach knot Kleenex
tissue abnormal tissue
weeping seeping creeping
needle punch gloved fist
KY glazed sweating grunting
       Relax, honey, this'll be quick
viral swarms hard cells violet stains
cold lonely drive useless arm numb
docetaxel paclitaxel cisplatin knife
radiation bald aching radio silence
pain ulcered tongue burnt Valentine
grave.

HER STORY OF CURLS
Lena Geneva Smith

EVERYONE WANTS CURLY HAIR, BUT NOT ME, OR AT LEAST I DIDN'T AS A CHILD. MY HAIR MADE DAILY ACTIVITIES COMPLICATED. I LEARNED THAT AS A CHILD PLAYING AT A FRIEND'S HOUSE.

IT WAS A WARM SUMMER DAY IN 1999.

Once I'm done you'll look great!

You're the best hairstylist around!

Hair 5 Salon

WHAT MY FRIEND DIDN'T UNDERSTAND IS MY HAIR EASILY KNOTS AND IT TAKES AN HOUR, AT THE LEAST, TO DO IT. EVERYDAY MY HAIR WAS IN BRAIDS. BRAIDS WERE THE ONLY WAY TO GO.

It's my turn to be the customer.

Well, what's stopping you?

If I leave the braids in, then mom won't have to do them again!

Okay, but I don't think it's a good idea.

IN THAT MOMENT, ALL I CARED ABOUT WAS HAVING FUN.

EVERYTHING WAS PERFECT... OR SO I THOUGHT.

What a mess, you have shampoo dried in you hair!

I REMEMBER HATING MY HAIR.

I REMEMBER THE TWO HOURS IT TOOK TO DETANGLE AND REMOVE THE DRIED SHAMPOO.

I REMEMBER GOING TO SCHOOL WITH MY HAIR STICKING OUT AS IF I'D BEEN SHOCKED, BECAUSE I'D ASKED MY MOM NOT TO RE-BRAID MY HAIR YET.

I LOOK BACK AT IT ALL AND SMILE. EVEN THOUGH MY HAIR CAN STILL BE FRUSTRATING, MY CURLS HAVE MADE ME WHO I AM, SOMEONE I CAN BE PROUD OF.

63

REVELING
Ryan Shepard

Sometimes he would sit for days
watching his brothers fight
the neighbors
or taunt the speeding traffic.
Grandma was kept inside,
in her wheelchair. To kill
an afternoon, he took a golf club
and smashed the garage windows,
finding life in the noise and shatter.
The walls were next.
He spent days with friends,
mauling the garage,
punching holes,
reveling,
until the building moaned
and slanted
towards the riverbank,
crushing his dog.
At the river
his friends found gasoline,
pulled up an old couch to the wreckage
and sat down
to watch it burn.
He stayed back at the bridge,
watching water churn
around others' garbage.

BREAKING LIGHT
Sheffield Reynolds

INTERSEXION
Loba Wakinyan

The wetlands are just outside my door   I walk
out   alone   under the cover of the Great Horned
Owl's hunt   Cap or hood pulled over my head
shoulders broad   pace long   swagger   and even
my comfort   show the few crepuscular walkers

                    Maleness
I speak to the woman walking past with a
quickening step   pulling her coat closed around
her   and staring at the cracks in the misplaced
asphalt   Her shoulders soften   her pace relaxes
her head rises   This is my intent

To give her the peace I lose in day walks   with
my short hair and soft facial skin   to offer her
the safety I feel under the cover of darkness and
butch build   to create safety for her through my
privileged disguise   brief and fleeting and
welcome

When the man comes by   I ignore him

                    He ignores me

LIGHTS, CAMERA, ACTION:
PLAYING WITH PERSPECTIVE
IN VIRGINIA WOOLF'S MRS. DALLOWAY
Meghan O'Neill

FADE IN.

INTRO: The writing of Virginia Woolf is famous for being consistently inconsistent. In all her work she fearlessly pushes the boundaries of literature and *Mrs. Dalloway* is no exception. She plays with perspective, time, and form. All within a story that takes place in the span of a single day in June and where the main plot topic is a high society party. Her experimentation creates an intimate world for the reader. A world where all the characters' minds are an open book and the reader can transition smoothly from one to the next like changing channels on a television. If Woolf had applied her genre-bending techniques to the film world, there would be an Oscar on her shelf.

CUT TO – NEXT PARAGRAPH: Setting the entirety of a novel within one day may seem lacking in subject matter, but Woolf flushes out many different and interesting storylines by manipulating the perspective. She smoothly transitions from the mind of one character to another and then another, sometimes within the span of a page. "'Look,' she implored him, for Dr. Holmes had told her to make him notice real things... 'Look,' she repeated. Look the unseen bade him, the voice which now communicated

with him who was the greatest of mankind..."
(25). The author carefully crafts each scene and
supplies them with multiple cameras, constantly
switching angles to portray the most alluring
story. These changeovers are so well executed that
the reader's experience is not interrupted in any
way. Woolf keeps the reader's attention on a
central focal point such as a location (Regent's
Park) or an event (a skywriting aeroplane). Many
characters provide insight or thoughts, "'That's an
E,' said Mrs. Bletchly – or a dancer- 'It's toffee,'
murmured Mr. Bowely" (21) before attention is
brought back around to the central character,
"'What are they all looking at?' said Clarissa
Dalloway to the maid who opened her door" (29).
The reader is able to gain up close and personal
knowledge of key characters while simultaneously
experiencing the big picture.

DISSOLVE TO INTERCUT – ADDITIONAL
INFORMATION: Another unique aspect to use
of varying perspectives is the ability to convey
what different characters are doing within the
same time period. This is extremely helpful when
the story takes place during the course of a single
day. It also provides an interesting 'real time'
reading experience to the reader. Woolf maintains
a consistent through line of marking time by the
chiming of Big Ben, something distinctly London
and heard by every character. "It was precisely
twelve o'clock; twelve by Big Ben; whose stroke
was wafted over the northern part of London..."
(94). Time seems to pass quickly for many of the
characters, "Three, good Heavens! Three already!

For with overpowering directness and dignity the clock struck three..." (118). By routinely referring back to the chiming of the clock, the reader does not become lost among the many minds and thoughts of various characters. The clock becomes another tool to act as a focal point in the same manner as a location or an event. It is only through the inclusion of these tactics that the reader is able to dive so deeply into the experiences of the characters without becoming lost.

CONTINUED: Woolf not only pushes the boundaries of perspective and timeline, but also the form of the novel itself. The entire work is written in one long, single section. No chapter breaks or sections. It has become common for stories to be written from multiple perspectives, however they usually alternate between different characters with each chapter. The chapters may even be titled with the specific character's name to avoid any and all confusion for the reader. It is amazing that Woolf is able to flow flawlessly between perspectives and within time without losing the reader's engagement or by using any type of formatting to provide structure. Especially since this novel is not a Kerouac stream-of-consciousness spewing of thoughts, but a carefully constructed scene played out with precise movements. In fact, the reader barely notices this lack of traditional structure.

CLOSE UP - TO SUMMARIZE: Reading Virginia Woolf is always a new adventure. She wields the conventional tools of fiction in completely new ways to create a rare and captivating novel each time. Readers are caught in the flow of the writing, swept away in the tide of the character's thoughts. The same way a great film director is able to manufacture a multi-dimensional story on screen, Woolf splendidly composes a multi-faceted tale within the pages of her novels.

FADE OUT.

THE END.

Woolf, Virginia. *Mrs. Dalloway*. New York: Harcourt, 1981. Print.

HIDDEN
Ryan Shepard

In the dark, a faint glow from the town;
I drive down roads in the calm
before the snowstorm
tapping presets while gripping the wheel.

AM radio, high on the dial
with the inconsequential topics
sparking the best arguments like we hear in
movies
or through neighbors' walls.

Angry words with random bursts of silence
punctuating, emphasizing
points of rumination, calculating
what else to cut with.

I never go to bed angry.
I go to bed tired. It's enough to rile anyone
itching for a fight so late into the evening.
In the dark, a faint glow

and now I scrape my blade
sparking
calculating what else to cut.

TAKE YOUR SHOES OFF
Sheffield Reynolds

HARDENED HANDS
Kristy Watson-Ables

Brenna didn't know her favorite part. The feeling of her feet sliding up her warm leg, cold toes brushing against the smoothness of her leg, the giggles that came from deep in her belly. The way her girlfriend's breath tickled against her ear, words lost, but a soft brush of air, the need to draw closer. She needed to feel this woman. Even if home had always been a place she could never land, she knew, this, their chests tight against each other, was home.

Could it always feel like this? She wasn't sure, and she was afraid, it couldn't, but it was now, and if it was now, could it be? Just be.

They hadn't planned to live together. Not here in her small studio apartment, bed fully in view of the front door, her schoolbooks stacked against the wall, Stacia's art supplies scattered across the kitchenette table. She'd always thought of home: a settled place in the suburbs, parents with children, two full-time jobs. Who were they, two college students floundering through the world, to fully believe they had found love?

Sometimes it was the outside that didn't feel real. The stark buildings, grey and hard, against her eyes and her fingers. She missed the feeling of her skin, the way Stacia's belly caved against her hands. Stacia's body in the dim light, naked skin glowing warm. Too beautiful to touch. Too irresistible to not feel. Stacia would smile, and whisper, come here. A lightness in her head, feelings that drugs could not replicate. The lines between their bodies blurred, stories merged. Her scars stolen into the smoothness of Stacia's skin.

She ran her hands along her body. The ridges of all the destruction she had left rough, she swallowed, ashamed.

"I don't care", Stacia murmured. Kissing her belly, kissing the purple streaks.

Brenna shook her head. Words caught beneath a lump in her throat. How someone could look at her body and feel love?

"I know you don't like to talk about it. Do you think you ever could?"

Brenna tipped her head. She could, she knew she could talk about it, but she wondered, if Stacia knew how deep the hate had run, could she still love? The knives had hid under her bed, in her underwear drawer, beneath the most personal things in her life, where she knew they wouldn't be discovered. Waiting for when she needed them, small saviors to draw her out of the moments she couldn't live through. The metal across her skin, hands hardened to doing what had to be done. She had closed her baby sister's ears to their parents' fights, to the sound of the gun shooting their injured cat, against the accusations of their mother, who said she would always be wrong. The hands she steadied against the cold blades, drew them across her skin, again and again, until her belly quivered, anguished, drawing the pain bottled inside of her chest, running down her skin, staining her jeans, crying out the tears that she always held in.

74

"I did it over and over." Brenna cried as Stacia held her head, tears against her warm hands. "I couldn't stop."

PANTING
Sheffield Reynolds

TAYLOR FARM ROAD
Jon Ulrich

The golden paper beech leaves shivering
At the ends of quiet branches
Dressed in green lichen,

Maple buds teased from their beds
By warm December days
Now left to die,

And wild turkeys
Scurrying across the hillside
Among truncated stalks of corn.

To the east, a mountain's crowning haze
And a raven's murderous call:

Winter is beautiful and terrifying.

Deceived by the mechanism of my own design,
I wonder if I have anything left to say that's worth
saying
And whether I belong
In this cold Vermont town

Or somewhere else.

Today I walked a country lane
Dappled with salt and sand
And the tracks of an Eastern cottontail
On its way to places unknown.

There is a dis-ease in my step
As I walk along slippery sheets of ice
On the shoulder
Of Taylor Farm Road.

GREYHOUND
Scott Morris

In this life of movement, I've found that
Greyhound stations are a lot more representative
of their respective cities than airports or plazas or
tourist brochures. Usually in the rougher part of
town, they are stuck far enough away (usually in
the neighborhood that has Army Reserve
billboards that list the exact dollar amount of the
enlistment bonus) that the land is cheap enough
to tolerate the ilk that many assume arrive via this
unique form of long haul migration.

I sit in the stiff metal seat, honestly trying to
avoid eye contact with all. This depot's setting is
exactly as I remember it: vending machines line
the west wall, filled with overpriced chips and
candy, the overtired travelers camped among
heaps of baggage. The only guard in the place is
stationed outside the bathroom, and I must show
him my ticket and ID before I am allowed a pre-
trip tinkle. The homeless line this guard's barrier,
envious of the privilege ticketed passengers may
luxuriate in. The last time I was here in this
Spartan room I was a young man, California-
bound. Now I think Salt Lake City might be my
begrudging home. At the very least it is a domicile
– the government issued ID I'll use to get on the
bus lists an address in Liberty Wells.

After my mandatory bathroom stop, I see a
man topping off a paper cup of water at the
drinking fountain which issues a horizontal
dribble. Cup full, he follows me at a trot back

towards the waiting area. Catching my eye, I can see this man is a long distance rider, fleeing from Corpus Christi or OKC towards points west, greener pastures. He wears a neck pillow as a permanent fixture and has baggy cotton hanging from every limb. He walks to the microwave, and I see him pull two bags from a large kangaroo pouch hidden in the folds of the hoodie. He opens a pouch of Fritos, a depot vending machine favorite, and pours them into an empty Ziploc as the water turns under the acrid radiation of the microwave. Upon the beep, he pours the water in and shakes the mixture. The man has my full attention, above the very important business of reshuffling my tickets and drinking water, but I don't think any other bleary-eyed riders are seeing this alchemy.

With a shuffle, he returns to his partner. Many things hang from her- a baby, rolls of flesh, a much too-large tee, and yellowed shards of teeth. He passes the bag to her, and, both wielding spoon shaped bits of plastic, they set to their work. She spoons the goop into the baby's mouth while he dabs some into a thick paste onto her leg as a poultice, where a recent tattoo oozed infection and smelt. Traveler's innovation?

I was called out of silent amazement by the shriek of the disgruntled rent-a-guard over a cheap PA system. Half the room stood up and started to gather around the door leading out to the bus. She got to the front of the mob and shouted at the assembled adults to form a single file line. She continued on in this shrill vein for what felt like a few minutes before the stiff-limbed people made any attempt at movement. Once we all realized that she wasn't going to let anybody on the bus until we lined up like good children, we shuffled into a more compact column. She then proceeded down towards me, holding everyone's ticket for a few seconds while looking down at her shoes. While she held mine I used the time to note her rotten teeth, her abundant perspiration and her generally hard-to-pin down body shape.

I was shuttled into a separate line, relegated to behind the reboarders who had been on since Denver. Joining the leg was only me and one other man, a compact *caballero* with sweat-stained cowboy hat and life-worn boots. Accompanying him was a wife, baby, and young son and their desperate clinging suggested they weren't coming along. When the reboarders started shuffling out the door, a tear hung from his proud cheek.

They were speaking Quechuan, which worked in my favor; when people speak languages I don't understand I get to translate it into whatever story I see fit. To my ear, He was headed to an apple orchard in Eastern Oregon, following the fall harvest. Things had been strained since their car had required a thousand bucks of repairs. He might have to go from there directly down to California for the following harvest, and not knowing when she would see him again was tearing Consuela apart. She hung onto him and cried until the man pulled from her and shuffled towards the bus.

The day before, a thick inversion had settled over the City. Due to the nature of the valley, the

Wasatch Front holds the pollution in a thick blanket overhead when differences in air pressure prevent movement of air. As we drove north past Ogden, I strained my gaze through haze, trying to spot an end to the gloom. Instead, I saw a brief orange blast. As we drew closer, I could see that the blasts were coming out of several large towers. A large factory a few miles back had been labeled "Deseret Mill and Pasta," so I wondered who was behind this shortsightedness. It seemed like a good metaphor for Utah today. I didn't see the sky until we crossed the Idaho border.

An hour before the border, the party started. The Frito-innovation couple had teamed up with two solo male travelers to form a bloc of revelers. The unmistakable pop and fizz of a cheap beer opening sounded from four pairs of hands in the two rows behind me. A vape was passed around. With only a tinge of marijuana smell, these devices had removed the necessity of getting stoned in the bus bathroom for the dedicated Greyhound long-hauler. I begrudged them only for the yelling, but that was mostly solved by headphones with Seattle-based hip hop artists, with the volume turned all the way up. I was no saint – I had a small pouch in my carry-on filled with hash-oil-laden peanut brittle.

By Twin Falls the drunkards were asleep while I was ensconced within the landscape the bus was moving through. It had been a hard four months in Salt Lake and on a quiet bus in a barren moonscape I was able to start the process of shedding that and striving towards the traveler's presence. Once fully absorbed into a trip, all the

82

ties to home and responsibility and worry are gradually left behind and the traveler is floating free in a vast sea – an unaffiliated vestige that can do nothing but observe and engage in this strange new world.

The plain of the Snake River stretched out past my window, framed by mountain ranges I didn't know the name of and may never. When I travel, I can't help but put myself in that space, but it's always the best version of me:

A long ridge leading up towards a summit - "If I lived here, I would run up that hill every day."

A beautiful farmhouse on the banks of the Snake – "If I had that place, I would write beautiful sentences all day long."

The bus rolled on as I continued to look out the window. The journal and the book sat on the seat next to me unused, despite the ambitious progress I had planned for both. I dreamed, and the bus motored on towards Boise. I was excited for this scheduled meal stop, because I had heard from several reputable sources that Boise, ID has the most beautiful women in the world.

As soon as they began their half hour fuel-and-clean, I struck out in pursuit of a Boise Beauty. I moved quickly, having prepared on the bus with a few pulls from my traveling flask at the city limits, hoping to take full advantage of the limited time. I set off quickly towards the lights and passed a few warmly lit bars full of hipsters. I had only gone four blocks when I saw her, heading in the other direction on the other side of the street. The quick glance from a distance was enough for me to detour towards her– I walked to the end of the street, crossed to her side, and initiated my chase.

Catching up near the intersection, I saw that her destination was the 10 Barrel Brewery. The front windows were generous, so I pretended to read the menu by the door while scanning for the woman who I was sure was destined to be my wife. I spotted her quickly and my initial interest was confirmed by this jacketlessness: Long limbed, full breasts, framed by platinum blonde hair that could only be compared to a South Dakota wheat harvest at the peak of plumpness, at sunset, after you'd eaten three 'special' mushrooms. I stood with my mouth open, unable to contain my love for her or prevent myself from picturing making tea for her while she sits on a rocking chair on the front porch of the retirement home we bought on the Maine coast. It took her seven, rapturous seconds to follow the host to the table, seven seconds that I belonged completely to her and her every desire. Seven seconds, and then the man she was meeting jumped up and embraced her passionately. My heart broke into a million little pieces and I walked back to the depot.

Around midnight I disembarked at Stanfield, OR. From what I saw, Stanfield is nothing but a gas station on the side of I-84. I had six hours there to wait for the morning bus to Seattle. Most passengers, including the partiers and poultice experts continued on into the moist night, towards Portland. I went into the McDonald's and appropriated a booth for my purposes. I again

84

employed my travel flask and, once used to a certain amount, I was able to transition into a kind of half-sleep. In this state you're still acutely aware of the discomfort of your body on the rigid plastic bench, but time seems to move a bit more quickly.

The morning bus was late, and the sun was up before I got on and folded myself into another seat. We left I-84 and headed north across the Columbia. The new sun was illuminating orchards on the banks of the river; a Rubicon of sorts, so I decided now was a good time for my edible treats. The best thing about this state legalizing marijuana was that instead of shoddy, home-spun edibles, everything was standardized and potent; after 20 minutes I was writing erotic poetry and staring lazily at the rolling patina, feeling good.

Rain beat heavily against the bus and we stopped in a few towns to pick up refugees bound for the big city. No thoughts of home and life at home, I was happy with what I was seeing. The green and the rain were as vivid as I had imagined and there was a scent on the air that was unfamiliar in acrid Utah: maybe musty dampness mixed with virility?

The bus struggled up Snoqualmie Pass just as the THC hit a crescendo. Towering Douglas Fir hung over entrenched banks of snow, and the rocky crags above dwarfed the large bus. We crested the pass and started down the other side. Straight down the hill lay the outer reaches of the city and beyond, the Puget Sound.

My last connection from Seattle was on a regional line that serviced the Olympic Peninsula.

This was a higher class route, which means the only difference was that instead of ignoring you over a cigarette, when the driver pulls up a half hour late he apologizes, and pretends to check your name against the manifest. As I settled into the rearmost seat for my final two hours – a scenic conclusion to 28 long hours – I spied a folder bearing the name of the conference I was headed for sitting on the bench next to the man across the aisle. Panicking, I shoved my notes and books back into the bag and put earbuds in, lest he rob me of my precious anonymity even a second earlier than as required by professional best practices.

HIS
Loba Wakinyan

You think my sex comes from yours   that this
means you possess me

My ribs are virgin unto themselves   they have
never been flesh of your flesh

bone of your bone   My womb creates blood
from blood   iron forged of a strength that you

long to claim dominion over   to rise up from
your place at the bottom of empty pockets

by claiming the power of my sex to create your
sex

Let me tell you this

       Sex is not unclean   mine nor yours
Sex is not a possession except

       to the one carrying it around with them
everywhere they go   Sex is not yours to steal

       or claim or rule from your self sanctioned
reign   Sex is not yours to penetrate at your

       own will

I do not consent and that is my right   never
belonging to you   My authority granted only to

those who share my lust for righteousness
possessed by the sea of lips   My waves crash

against the shore of another myself   and this
erects your rage   which you attempt to publicly

ejaculate onto my house   but my audacity to
remain turned on by

                    the reaches of my own hand

renders you impotent

CONTRIBUTORS

SARAH RATERMANN BEAHAN is an MFA candidate at Goddard College. After traveling around the United States looking for a place to call home, she now resides in Minneapolis, Minnesota where she writes and teaches. She chronicles her adventures at www.greatbeahanadventure.com. Previous literary accolades include editing The Pitkin Review, writing an entertainment blog for The St. Louis Post-Dispatch, production of her play Gas'n'Go at the Webster University Conservatory Theatre and cleverly written Facebook status updates.

ANNIE GALLIGAN is a 17 year-old who writes autobiographical musings in the hopes that it will remind her she's actually 33. Her writing process involves dreaming up poignant, lyrical prose in the shower, and forgetting it before she has time to dry off and find a pen. Annie spends her time between Maine and Rhode Island, with a dog who is a great man, and a great man who is the best part of every story. Her writing has been read and liked by thousands; the entirety of her published work may be found on Facebook.com.

SCOTT MORRIS is an outdoor educator, runner, and writer currently splitting his time between Salt Lake City and the Sierra Nevada of California.

MEGHAN O'NEILL, a mountain biker and avid book nerd, has yet to successfully combine her passions (although many scraped knees and ripped pages haven't impeded her efforts). Living in beautiful British Columbia, Canada Meghan can't wait to escape outside. She spends most of her time tackling trails with her bike or curled up in the sun with her latest book. Either way, her 105-pound dog Lexa is never far away. Meghan's future goals include: putting away her laundry, learning how to change a bike tire, and finishing her Masters degree in creative writing.

JALYN POWELL is an 8th grade English teacher in Midland, Texas, where she tries to spread the word on the finer aspects of grammar and innate goodness of books to America's youth. She writes science fiction, fantasy, and everything in between. Her work has appeared in The TU Review and will soon be produced on The Overcast.

SHEF REYNOLDS makes pictures and poems. You can find more of his work at shefreynolds.com.

JONATHAN RYDER grew up on Cape Cod where he quickly was drawn to poetry due to the rich natural landscape. During his undergraduate studies at Roger Williams University he focused on learning the craft of poetry and experimenting with other genres before finally being drawn to fiction. Currently, he is pursuing a masters program at Goddard College which focuses on fiction, yet continues writing poetry and seeks to meld poetic language into his fiction.

RYAN SHEPARD is a poet that treats many symptoms of boredom. Ryan Shepard is not approved for children under 18. Side effects may include interest, renewed inspiration, the urge to Google something online, a craving for books, and the want of a good Coltrane album. Ask your bookstore if Ryan Shepard is right for you.

LAURA SCHAEFFER's poetry is an exploration into absence and those transcendencies of emotion and experience that lift into borderless realms that can only be defined through the sensory in our physical world. Rainer Maria Rilke and Mahmoud Darwish have had a profound impact on her writing, as has the landscape of her rural home in the Pacific Northwest.

JOHN SCHMIDTKE lives in Hawaii. Most mornings, he daydreams at his keyboard as the sun crests the silhouette of Molokai and turns the waters of the Kaiwi Channel from coal and lead to silver and gold. And then, sometimes, he starts writing.

TANYA SEALE writes fiction and plays for adults and young adults. Her plays have been produced in St. Louis, MO and Houston, TX. Her poems, stories, and nonfiction for very young readers have been published in *Highlights for Children, Humpty Dumpty's Magazine, Fun for Kidz, Hopscotch for Girls, Spider*, and others. You can find her online at tgseale.com.

LENA GENEVA SMITH is a young adult fiction writer and graphic novel artist from Ohio. She is also an ASL interpreter and tennis coach for Westerville Special Olympics. She has aspirations to become a mermaid and her secret identity is Luna Lovegood! She loves her friends, family, and God. This is her first publication! Woot woot!

LUCY A. SNYDER is a four-time Bram Stoker Award-winning writer. Her most recent books include the story collections "While the Black Stars Burn" and "Soft Apocalypses." Her writing has been translated into French, Russian, Italian, Czech, and Japanese editions and has appeared in a wide variety of publications. She lives in Columbus, Ohio. You can learn more about her at lucysnyder.com and you can follow her on Twitter at @LucyASnyder.

TERISA TRAYLOR is a Seattle native currently living in Atlanta, Georgia while working on her poetry manuscript "The Wounds That Bind Us." Terisa uses her experiences of grief, loss, and love to create unity between her poems and the human experience of suffering and growth. Terisa teaches a weekly poetry class at a homeless youth shelter in Atlanta and aspires to create more opportunities for her to teach poetry to youth as a form of healing and empowerment.

JON ULRICH graduated cum laude from the State University of New York at Oswego with a degree in communications. His writing has appeared in Life in the Finger Lakes magazine,

Conservationist, and Adirondack Life. Jon's first book, Winter in the Wilderness, is now available from Comstock Publishing Associates, and imprint of Cornell University Press. He lives in Newfield, New York with his wife, Laura, and children, Graham and Elliott.

LOBA WAKINYAN is a Heyoka, better known as Coyote, who dares to feed on the flesh of ignorance and beauty; an explorer navigated by their own compass, sometimes pointing them right, but always directing them left. Loba writes to flip the comfortable inside out, to view the intestines of a subject and spray them across a canvas to force our eyes to widen, becoming more honest and humble at once.

KRISTY WATSON-ABLES is a sign language interpreter, college instructor, and writer living in Columbus, Ohio. She enjoys an unending cup of coffee, cuddling with her cats, and creating artistic messes.

57813564R00054

Made in the USA
Charleston, SC
22 June 2016